Ecosystems
Tundras

Erinn Banting

www.av2books.com

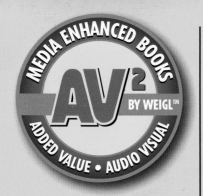

AV² provides enriched content that supplements and complements this book. Weigl's AV² books strive to create inspired learning and engage young minds in a total learning experience.

Your AV² Media Enhanced books come alive with...

Audio
Listen to sections of the book read aloud.

Key Words
Study vocabulary, and complete a matching word activity.

Go to **www.av2books.com**, and enter this book's unique code.

Video
Watch informative video clips.

Quizzes
Test your knowledge.

BOOK CODE

D 6 7 9 8 8 5

Embedded Weblinks
Gain additional information for research.

Slide Show
View images and captions, and prepare a presentation.

AV² by Weigl brings you media enhanced books that support active learning.

Try This!
Complete activities and hands-on experiments.

... and much, much more!

Published by AV² by Weigl
350 5th Avenue, 59th Floor
New York, NY 10118
Website: www.av2books.com   www.weigl.com

Library of Congress Cataloging-in-Publication Data

Banting, Erinn.
 Tundras / Erinn Banting.
     p. cm. -- (Ecosystems)
 Includes bibliographical references and index.
 ISBN 978-1-61913-075-3 (hard cover : alk. paper) -- ISBN 978-1-61913-238-2 (soft cover : alk. paper)
 1. Tundra ecology--Juvenile literature. I. Title.
 QH541.5.T8B36 2013
 577.5'86--dc23
                            2011045202

Printed in the United States of America in North Mankato, Minnesota
1 2 3 4 5 6 7 8 9 16 15 14 13 12

012012
WEP060112

Project Coordinator Aaron Carr
Design Sonja Vogel

Every reasonable effort has been made to trace ownership and to obtain permission to reprint copyright material. The publishers would be pleased to have any errors or omissions brought to their attention so that they may be corrected in subsequent printings.

Photo Credits
Weigl acknowledges Getty Images as its primary photo supplier for this title.

Contents

What is a Tundra Ecosystem?

The word *tundra* comes from the Russian word for barren land. The frozen ground in tundra ecosystems cannot support trees or other large plants.

Earth is home to millions of different **organisms**, all of which have specific survival needs. These organisms rely on their environment, or the place where they live, for their survival. All plants and animals have relationships with their environment. They interact with the environment itself, as well as the other plants and animals within the environment. These interactions create **ecosystems**.

Tundras are regions in the coldest places on Earth. There are two types of tundra. Arctic tundra is found mainly in the far north of the northern **hemisphere**, such as near the North Pole. Alpine tundra is found on high mountains all over the world, including the Swiss Alps. Tundras have low temperatures, little precipitation, and short growing seasons. Plants and animals have been forced to adapt to these difficult conditions in order to survive.

Though tundras may seem lifeless, they are home to some of the most interesting plants and animals on Earth. Plants found in tundras include tundra poppies and lichens. Polar bears and caribou are just two kinds of animal found in the tundra.

Levels of Organization in Tundra Ecosystems

Organizing the Tundra

Ecosystems can be broken down into levels of organization. These levels range from a single plant or animal to many **species** of plants and animals living together in an area.

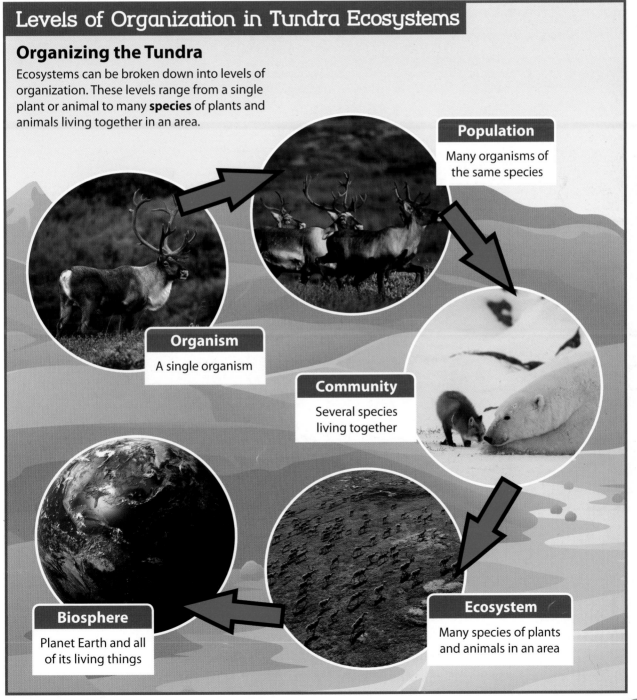

Population

Many organisms of the same species

Organism

A single organism

Community

Several species living together

Ecosystem

Many species of plants and animals in an area

Biosphere

Planet Earth and all of its living things

Where in the World?

Denali National Park in Alaska protects about 9,420 square miles (24,938 square kilometers) of tundra ecosystem. This is an area larger than the state of Massachusetts.

Tundra ecosystems are found in the most northern parts of the world. They also occur in some parts of Antarctica and on high mountain peaks. In these areas, temperatures remain below freezing most of the year. The ground beneath the Arctic tundra is always frozen. This permanently frozen ground is called permafrost. It is difficult for trees and plants to grow in these conditions.

Polar Tundras

Tundra covers about 20 percent of Earth's surface. The largest area of tundra is the Arctic tundra zone. This zone covers the most northern reaches of North America, Europe, and Asia. North America's tundra region stretches from north of Alaska and Canada to the easternmost part of Greenland. The far north region of Europe, which includes Scandinavia and Iceland, is also part of the Arctic tundra. In Asia, the tundra stretches from the coast of the Arctic Ocean in Russia to Siberia in the east. Antarctica is Earth's southernmost point. There is a tundra region on the Antarctic Peninsula, as well as on several of the islands surrounding the continent, including South Georgia.

Eco Facts

The word *Himalaya* comes from an ancient language called Sanskrit, and means "abode of snow." The Himalayan mountain range was named after its peaks, which are the tallest in the world and are covered with snow year-round.

Tundras in the Mountains

Tundra can also be found in higher **altitudes**. Alpine tundra is located throughout the mountain ranges of western North America, as well as the Andes Mountains of South America. Other alpine tundras are located in the central European Alps and the Himalayas, a mountain range that stretches throughout Asia.

| In the North American Rocky Mountains, tundras usually occur at altitudes above 11,000 feet (3,353 meters). |

Tundra ecosystems are found in specific parts of the world. This map shows where the world's major tundra areas are located. Find the place where you live on the map. Do you live near a tundra ecosystem? If not, which tundra area is closest to you? Why do you think tundra is located only in certain parts of the world?

Legend

- Arctic Tundra
- Alpine Tundra
- Ocean
- River

Scale at Equator

| 0 | 1,000 | 2,000 | 3,000 miles |

| 0 | 1,000 | 2,000 | 3,000 kilometers |

N

ARCTIC OCEAN

Rocky Mountains, United States and Canada

NORTH AMERICA

Cascade Mountains, United States and Canada

ATLANTIC OCEAN

EQUATOR

SOUTH AMERICA

PACIFIC OCEAN

North American Tundra

Location: North America (United States, Canada, Greenland)
Size: 1.6 million square miles (4.2 million sq. km)
Fact: In North America, the tundra ecosystem is found along the coast of Greenland and across northern Canada and Alaska. Much of the land in the **Arctic Circle** is covered in permafrost. In northern Alaska, the permafrost layer can be as deep as 2,428 feet (740 meters).

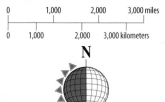

Andes Mountains

Location: South America (Argentina, Chile)
Height: Above 11,500 feet (3,500 meters) in the north and at sea level at the southern tip of the continent
Fact: The Andes mountain system contains a series of high plateaus and even higher peaks. It forms an unbroken chain that spans a distance of 5,500 miles (8,850 km). The mountain chain stretches from the southern tip of South America to the northernmost coast of the continent. The highest peaks remain covered in snow and ice year-round. The average annual temperature in the Andean tundra is 50° Fahrenheit (10° Celsius).

ARCTIC OCEAN

The Pyrenees,
France, Spain,
and Andorra

ASIA

EUROPE

The Himalayas,
Nepal, India, Pakistan, China,
Bhutan, Myanmar, Afghanistan

Eurasian Tundra

Location: Europe and Asia
(Russia, Scandinavia, Iceland)
Size: 1.5 million square miles
(4 million sq. km)
Fact: The Eurasian tundra covers
about 3 percent of Europe and
Asia's landmass. Almost half
of this ecosystem is located in
northern Russia. Precipitation
in this area is less than 15 inches
(38 centimeters) per year.
In northern Siberia,
the permafrost can
reach a depth
of 5,000 feet
(1,500 m) below
the surface.

Mount Kilimanjaro,
Tanzania

AFRICA

INDIAN
OCEAN

The Alps

Location: Europe (Central Europe)
Height: Between 5,000 and 9,000 feet
(1,524 and 2,743 m)
Fact: The Alps mountain range extends in an arc across
central Europe, from the Gulf of Genoa to the Danube
River. The 750-mile (1,200-km) mountain range covers
parts of 11 European countries. Alpine tundra in the Alps
occurs above 5,900 feet (1,800 m). This area is home
to many plants, such as creeping pine and dwarf
shrubs, and animals, including ibex, chamois,
and the alpine daw. About 2 percent of
the total area of the Alps is covered by ice.
These ice-covered, or glaciated, areas are
located above the tundra zone, usually at
elevations above 9,800 feet (3,000 m).

SOUTHERN
OCEAN

ANTARCTICA

9

Tundra Climates

Tundra ecosystems usually receive less than 14 inches (36 centimeters) of precipitation each year. This is similar to many desert ecosystems.

The tundra ecosystem climate is characterized by fast-moving winds, snow, ice, and freezing temperatures. These regions also experience very short summers. When the Sun shines, plants sprout from the ground, and animals hunt for food for the winter.

The tundra is a land of extremes. Winters in the tundra begin in September and last up to nine months. Depending on where the tundra is located, winters can experience temperatures between 18° and –40° Fahrenheit (8° and –40° Celsius). Though temperatures rarely rise above 50°F (10°C), some tundra areas experience up to four months of summer weather. Summer temperatures in the tundra can change quickly. The average summer temperature is about 32°F (0°C).

Constant Change

Tundra ecosystems are always shifting, moving, and changing. Elements such as sunlight, glaciers, wind, and precipitation have helped form the tundra over millions of years.

Sunlight

Tundras can be characterized by the amount of light they receive from the Sun. Earth spins on a tilted **axis**. This means the Sun's rays never shine directly on the North Pole. In winter, the North Pole is far away from the Sun. During this time, the Sun never rises above the horizon in the Arctic tundras. Darkness lasts for 24 hours. In summer, the North Pole is closer to the Sun. At these times, the Sun never sets.

Glaciers

Glaciers are large, slow-moving masses of snow and ice. During the last major Ice Age, between 2 million and 10,000 years ago, glaciers covered much of Earth. About 10,000 years ago, Earth's temperature began to rise. Huge chunks of ice broke away and began to drift southward over the land. Glaciers moved soil, deposited rock, and flattened the tundra landscape. Glaciers continue to move across the tundra, keeping the land flat.

Wind

In some tundra regions, winds can reach up to 86 miles (140 km) per hour. Trees do not grow in Arctic tundra zones, so winds gather speed as they whip snow, ice, rocks, and the seeds of plants across the flat landscape.

Precipitation

Ice, snow, and water cause the tundra to shift and change. When water melts in the tundra, it is often trapped beneath the soil or in shallow pools or lakes. Water that does not evaporate freezes when temperatures drop. When water freezes, it expands. This creates cracks in the surface of the land.

Eco Facts

In Siberia, rivers freeze so thick the ice is strong enough to hold the weight of cars and trucks. People use the rivers as roadways during winter.

Icebergs are enormous chunks of ice that have broken away from glaciers. As they move toward the ocean, icebergs carve the tundra coastline.

Types of Tundra

Lichens and mosses are among the few plants suited to the cold temperatures and frozen ground of tundra ecosystems.

Tundras are divided by their geographic location into two types, Arctic tundra and alpine tundra.

Arctic Tundra

Arctic tundra ecosystems are found mainly around the North Pole. This includes parts of North America, Europe, and Asia. In the Arctic tundra, plants can only grow for 50 to 60 days. Plants with roots have difficulty growing in the thick permafrost. The growing season occurs in summer, when the ground's top layer is less frozen. Rainwater and meltwater, or water from melted snow and ice, gathers in ponds or **bogs**. This water helps the plants in the ecosystem grow.

Alpine Tundra

Alpine tundra ecosystems are found near the top of tall mountains. The growing season in these regions can last for 180 days. Some tree species, including dwarf trees, grow in alpine tundras. Temperatures in alpine tundras are very cold, and winds move at high speeds. Meltwater drains into mountain streams that carry the water to lower mountain regions.

Eco Facts

The tundra begins on the border of another ecosystem called the boreal forest, or taiga. This is an evergreen forest **biome** found in cold climates.

Tundra Features

Wetlands, polygons, and pingos are common land formations found in tundra ecosystems.

Wetlands

In the Arctic tundra, large areas become wet and swampy during summer. Meltwater cannot drain properly on the tundra's flat land. Instead, it becomes trapped in pools. The water does not absorb into the frozen ground. Water from some pools evaporates or is used by plants. Deeper pools form wetland areas and shallow lakes, which freeze during winter.

Pingos

Pingos are giant mounds of soil and decaying plant matter that grow up to 100 feet (30 m) high and 1,000 feet (305 m) wide. Pingos form when plants die in lakes that trap meltwater. In winter, the lakes freeze and expand, causing the dead plants and soil to rise to the surface. Each year, a new layer of trapped water, plants, and soil builds over the previous layer.

Polygons

Polygons are giant cracks in the tundra's surface. They are named after the five-sided shape they resemble. Polygons form over many years. In summer, the soil thaws, and the earth expands and contracts. This causes cracks to form. These cracks fill with water. In winter, the water freezes and expands. Ice is forced aboveground. Over time, a network of shallow cracks forms across the surface of the tundra.

Polygons similar to those found in the tundra also occur in the desert ecosystem of Death Valley, California.

Life in the Tundra

Harsh temperatures, winds, and a lack of precipitation make it difficult for plants and animals to survive in tundras. Still, these ecosystems are home to tens of thousands of unique plants and animals, many of which are not found in any other ecosystem.

Producers

The plants found in tundras act as producers for other organisms in the ecosystem. These organisms are called producers because they make their own food. They also serve as food for other organisms. Producers absorb energy from the Sun and convert it into usable forms of energy such as sugar. They make this energy through a process called **photosynthesis**. Producers found in tundras include lichens, mosses, some types of grass, and various shrubs.

Primary Consumers

The animals that rely on producers as a food source are called primary consumers. When a primary consumer feeds on a producer, the energy made by the producer is transferred to the consumer. Examples of primary consumers found in tundra ecosystems include several kinds of deer, such as caribou and moose, and many small mammals, including lemmings, pikas, and Arctic hares. Some insects, such as mosquitoes and black flies, can also be also primary consumers.

Tundra Energy Pyramid

The transfer of energy in an ecosystem begins with producers and moves up the energy pyramid to the tertiary consumers. Organisms at each level of the pyramid receive energy from the organisms in the level below them.

Outside of the pyramid are the decomposers. They break down the dead and decaying **organic** matter left behind when plants and animals die. For this reason, decomposers receive energy from organisms in all levels of the energy pyramid.

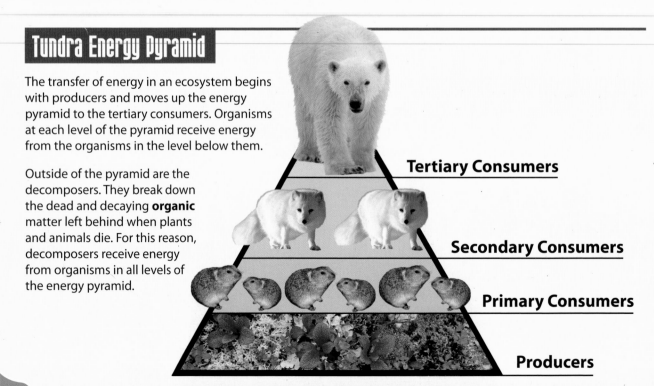

Tertiary Consumers

Secondary Consumers

Primary Consumers

Producers

Tundra Food Web

Another way to study the flow of energy through an ecosystem is by examining food chains and food webs. A food chain shows how a producer feeds a primary consumer, which then feeds a secondary consumer, and so on. However, most organisms feed on many different food sources. This practice causes food chains to interconnect, creating a food web.

In this example, the **red line** represents one food chain from the caribou lichen, muskox, and Arctic wolf. The blue line from the saxifrage to the Arctic hare, the Arctic fox, and the Arctic wolf forms another food chain. These food chains connect at the Arctic wolf, but they also connect in other places. The muskox also feeds from saxifrage, and the Arctic hare also eats caribou lichen. This series of connections forms a complex food web.

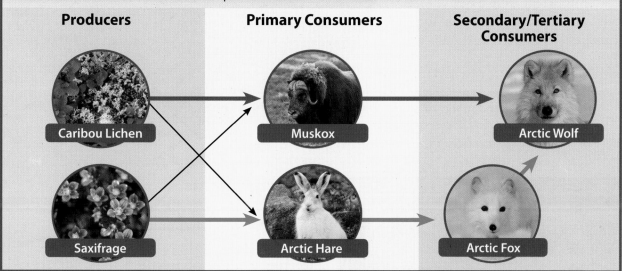

Producers	Primary Consumers	Secondary/Tertiary Consumers
Caribou Lichen	Muskox	Arctic Wolf
Saxifrage	Arctic Hare	Arctic Fox

Secondary and Tertiary Consumers

Secondary consumers feed on both producers and primary consumers. In the tundra, secondary consumers include foxes and brown bears. Larger carnivores, such as polar bears, and some large birds, including the snowy owl, are called tertiary consumers. Tertiary consumers feed on secondary consumers.

Decomposers

Fungi, such as Arctic mushrooms, and many types of bacteria live in tundra ecosystems. These organisms are called decomposers because they eat dead and decaying organic materials. Decomposers speed up the process of breaking down dead organic materials and releasing their **nutrients** into the soil. These nutrients are then absorbed by the roots of the plants living in the ecosystem.

Plants

Lichens

Tundra ecosystems are home to about 600 plant species. Lichens are plantlike organisms made up of **algae** and **fungi**. Lichens have no roots. This allows them to grow on the rocky surface of the tundra. Lichens look like orange, red, green, black, gray, or white splotches on the dark tundra floor. Caribou lichen is an important source of food for caribou. Lichen can grow up to 4 inches (10 centimeters) tall.

Lichens are highly adaptable organisms that can grow on soil, dirt, rock, or even permafrost.

Flowering Plants

There are about 250,000 species of flowering plant in the world, but only 500 of these live in tundra ecosystems. During summer, flowering plants wash the tundra in color. As the weather warms, the top layer of soil thaws, allowing flowers to take root. Many flowers grow in the tundra, including Arctic lupine, saxifrage, and yellow poppies. These flowers grow close to the ground or closely together so that heat from the soil does not escape. Their bright red, orange, blue, and pink colors attract insects. This helps the flowers spread the **pollen** and seeds they need to survive from year to year.

Animals in the tundra depend on the many berries that grow in the ecosystem, including blueberries and bearberries.

Arctic Cotton

Most tundra plants grow low to the ground. This protects the plants from cold temperatures and strong winds that can uproot them. Arctic cotton, a type of grass that can grow up to 1 foot (30 cm) tall, sways in the cold tundra breezes. This grass has puffy white cotton at its tips. People who live in tundra ecosystems collect this cotton and use it to insulate, or trap heat in, their boots, gloves, and other clothing.

Eco Facts

The area that separates forest from tundra is called the tree line. The tree line marks the point where it is too cold for trees to grow.

Plants prevent permafrost from melting. They protect the frozen ground from warmer temperatures and sunlight.

Shrubs

Shrubs are common in alpine tundra regions and the more southerly regions of the Arctic tundra. Bearberries are low shrubs that have bright red berries. The shrubs get their name because bears eat their fruit.

In tundra ecosystems, shrubs such as the Arctic willow often grow close to other plants, including moss and other shrubs.

Mammals

Polar Bears

Polar bears are easily recognized by their cream-colored coats. Weighing up to 990 pounds (450 kilograms), polar bears are the world's largest land carnivores, or meat-eating animals. They have developed special ways to stay warm in this frozen climate. Beneath their thick fur, polar bears have a 3-inch (8-cm) thick layer of blubber, or fat, that keeps them from becoming too cold. Like other tundra mammals, polar bears have found ways to survive in the extreme conditions of this ecosystem. Some polar bears **hibernate** to save energy during the coldest times of the year, when food is scarce. All pregnant females hibernate. They can go up to eight months without eating.

Polar bears spend much of their time on sea ice hunting for seals. Thick, rough pads on the bottom of their paws keep them from slipping on the ice.

Wolves

Where there is a herd of caribou, a pack of wolves is never far behind. A full-grown Arctic wolf stands 3 feet (91 cm) tall and weighs about 175 pounds (79 kg). Arctic wolves only kill what they can eat. Caribou are their main prey, but they also eat lemmings, Arctic hares, and muskoxen. Arctic wolves store food in their stomachs. This food is then **regurgitated** to feed their young.

Arctic wolves often hunt alone for small prey, but they will gather in packs of up to 30 to capture larger prey.

Lemmings

Lemmings are small, mouse-like creatures. They range from 3 to 6 inches (8 to 15 cm) long and weigh 0.5 to 4 ounces (14 to 113 grams). Lemmings burrow in tunnels underground. When food is scarce, lemmings leave their tunnels to move to another region. They run across the tundra in large groups, refusing to stop. They do not even eat during their migration. They swim across water, such as streams or rivers. Sometimes, lemmings try to cross the ocean. They often climb over top of each other in the process. Many lemmings drown as a result.

Eco Facts

Muskoxen have long, shaggy coats to keep them warm. They also have long, pointed horns to protect them from predators. Though muskoxen look like buffalo, they are actually related to goats.

The Arctic fox digs a den underground to protect itself from the harsh tundra climate.

Caribou

Caribou belong to the deer family. They are sometimes called reindeer. Caribou live in huge herds. They constantly **migrate** over long distances to avoid cold or to look for food. Each summer, caribou herds travel more than 600 miles (965 km) from the forests in the south to the tundra in the north. Caribou have thick fur coats that keep them warm. Each of their hairs is hollow. These hollow hairs help trap warmth from their bodies to keep the caribou from freezing.

Caribou come to the tundra to feed on the many plants that thrive during the summer months.

Birds, Insects, Whales, and Fish

Throughout the northern hemisphere, the kittiwake can be found nesting on cliffs along the seashore. Unlike other gulls, these birds rarely travel inland.

Birds

During summer, tundra ecosystems are home to thousands of migratory birds, including ducks, owls, sandpipers, and plovers. During winter, most birds fly to warmer climates. They return again the following summer. Few birds live in tundra regions year-round. Gulls and ravens brave the tundra cold all year. The ptarmigan is another bird that lives in the tundra throughout the year. About the size of a small chicken, the ptarmigan has a stout body, short tail and legs, and short, rounded wings. The ptarmigan is covered with feathers, even on its beak and feet. Foot feathers help the bird walk on top of soft snow. Other birds, such as the Arctic tern, arrive in spring and migrate to South America in winter.

Insects

A few insect species, including black flies, deer flies, and mosquitoes, call the tundra home. To keep from freezing, some insects replace their body's water with an antifreeze substance called glycerol. In the summer, black flies and mosquitoes swarm above warm, damp tundra wetland areas. Insects provide food for birds and other animals. They are important to life in tundra ecosystems.

A mosquito's mouth is a long, thin tube. It is used to eat nectar from flowers. Adult females use this tube to suck blood from animals.

Fish

There are few species of fish in tundra ecosystems because there is so little unfrozen water. The fish that live in these areas have adapted to their surroundings. The Alaska blackfish, which is found in North America and parts of Asia, can breathe air. This allows it to live in very little water.

Whales

The waters surrounding the Arctic tundra are filled with whales and other marine mammals that do not mind the freezing-cold surface temperatures. Water in the Arctic Ocean is also very cold, but whales have thick layers of blubber to keep them warm. Beluga and orca whales breach, or come above water for air, in the Arctic Ocean off the coast of the tundra. Orcas are sometimes called killer whales, even though they are not likely to harm humans. The nickname comes from their scientific name Orcinus orca. In Latin, *orcinus* means "bringer of death." Most whales feed on fish and plankton, which are very small organisms found in oceans.

Orcas are the largest members of the dolphin family. They feed on marine mammals, including seals and sea lions.

Tundra in Danger

The plants and animals that live in tundra ecosystems seem very strong, since they have adapted to harsh weather, extreme temperatures, and a lack of constant food sources. However, tundra regions are fragile, and many of the animals that call this ecosystem home are **endangered**.

Hunting is one of the biggest threats to the animals of tundra ecosystems. Polar bears are enormous and can run quickly, but hunters that want their fur have greatly reduced this animal's numbers. Muskoxen have been endangered more than once. In the 1900s, the large beasts were hunted for their meat, horns, and coats. By 1917, there were only a few hundred of the animals left. Since then, laws have been passed to protect these animals.

Pollution caused by human development and industries also harms tundra ecosystems. Pollution damages the tundra in the form of acid rain. Harmful chemicals become trapped in the rain. These chemicals poison plants and animals that need water to survive. Pollution also contributes to **global warming**. Many of the tundra's plants and animals can only survive in a cold environment. If Earth warms too much, some of these organisms will disappear. Scientists warn that global warming is causing much of the Arctic ice to melt. This reduces the natural habitat for many Arctic animals, including polar bears.

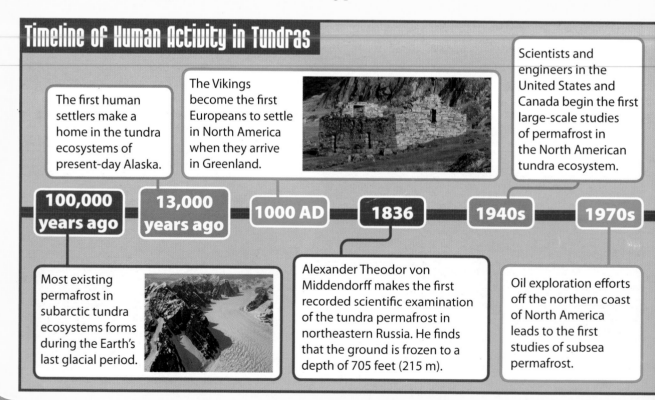

Timeline of Human Activity in Tundras

The first human settlers make a home in the tundra ecosystems of present-day Alaska.

The Vikings become the first Europeans to settle in North America when they arrive in Greenland.

Scientists and engineers in the United States and Canada begin the first large-scale studies of permafrost in the North American tundra ecosystem.

100,000 years ago | **13,000 years ago** | **1000 AD** | **1836** | **1940s** | **1970s**

Most existing permafrost in subarctic tundra ecosystems forms during the Earth's last glacial period.

Alexander Theodor von Middendorff makes the first recorded scientific examination of the tundra permafrost in northeastern Russia. He finds that the ground is frozen to a depth of 705 feet (215 m).

Oil exploration efforts off the northern coast of North America leads to the first studies of subsea permafrost.

The northern fur seal was hunted almost to extinction in the 19th century, but this marine mammal has rebounded with the help of protection laws. There are now more than one million fur seals in the world.

Engineers in Russia, China, and Scandinavia begin researching engineering techniques that will allow houses and other structures to be built in alpine tundra.

Researchers find that rising temperatures throughout Europe are increasing the risk of thawing the permafrost that holds together many of the mountain surfaces in the Alps.

Global warming over the previous decade causes drier conditions in the Alaskan tundra. From 2000 to 2010, lightning caused wildfires that burned more of the tundra than all of the wildfires that occurred from 1950 to 2000 combined.

1970s-80s | **1990s-2000s** | **2000** | **2001** | **2006** | **2010**

Increased mining and oil excavation activity in the Arctic tundra strains the ecosystem with higher pollution levels and less natural habitat for the plant and animal species of the area.

Satellite imagery shows that between 1982 and 2002, Arctic tundra has decreased in size by 18 percent.

An Alaskan oil pipeline leaks for five days before anyone notices the spill. More than 267,000 gallons (1 million liters) of oil covers an area of about 2 acres (0.8 hectares).

Science in the Tundra

Studying samples of water, ice, or snow can help scientists monitor changing levels of greenhouse gases.

One of the greatest dangers faced by tundra ecosystems is global warming. Global warming occurs when **greenhouse gases** in Earth's atmosphere trap heat from the Sun. This raises the temperature on the planet. Over the past 100 years, Earth's average temperature has risen 1°F (0.56°C). This increase has had a negative impact on tundra ecosystems.

Polar Icecaps

The coldest places on Earth are the first to experience the negative effects of global warming. Polar icecaps are large glaciers at the northernmost part of Earth. Heat from global warming could melt the polar icecaps. If these icecaps melt completely, the oceans will rise, changing the land humans, plants, and animals inhabit. It is important that tundra ecosystems remain barren, frozen places.

Studying the Tundra

The tundra acts as an important laboratory for scientists who study the effects of global warming. Scientists measure the climate, weather, and the rate at which glaciers and permafrost are melting. Scientists use weather stations, weather balloons, and ocean buoys to monitor tundra temperatures. Weather stations record daily temperatures, storms, and other clues to help scientists measure activity in the tundra. Weather balloons calculate gas levels in Earth's atmosphere. Ocean buoys take the temperature of the surrounding water. They also measure water levels and can alert scientists if there are any changes. All three of these tools provide important information to scientists from some of the coldest and most dangerous parts of the tundra.

Eco Facts

Scientists also study the effects of global warming on the creatures of the tundra. Experiments and long-term studies have focused on animals as large as the polar bear and as small as the nematode worm.

Soil and Ice

Other scientists study the soil and surface of tundra ecosystems. Scientists can analyze a soil sample to determine how fast glaciers are melting. They also use large drills to cut pieces of glaciers or layers of permafrost. From these samples, scientists can learn a great deal about the history of the tundra climate.

Scientists who study tundra ecosystems have to be able to work in extreme environments.

Working in the Tundra

Scientist studying glaciers often use global positioning system (GPS) devices to track glacier movement.

The people who study the land, plants, and animals of tundra ecosystems must have a strong background in history, math, and science. There are many types of jobs that involve studying the tundra, including **anthropology**, biology, and **paleontology**. Many people who work in the tundra study ecology.

Research Scientist

Duties

Studies tundra ecosystems, and collects and records data about the region's environment

Education

Bachelor of science or masters of science degree

Interests

Earth science, ecology, geology, biology, statistics

Research scientists study the plants, animals, and climates of tundra ecosystems. They work with assistants to find ways to protect the living creatures that call the tundra home. For example, these scientist track the migration patterns of animals such as caribou and birds. Research scientists also study the effects of global warming on the tundra's permafrost layer.

Other Tundra Jobs

Environmental Consultant

Studies how humans interact with tundras and the environment and looks for ways to protect these ecosystems

Biologist

Studies the plant and animal life found in tundras and anything that affects the natural balance in the ecosystem

Professor

Teaches students about ecosystems and various scientific fields, such as biology and ecology

Andrew Derocher

Andrew Derocher (1960–) is an ecologist and conservationist best known for his work studying polar bears on the tundra and icecaps of the Arctic. Derocher has spent nearly 30 years studying polar bears, their habitat, and the environment in which they live.

Derocher received a bachelor's degree in science in 1983. In 1991, he earned a doctoral degree from the University of Alberta in Edmonton, Canada. He worked with the Canadian government's environmental department before heading to Norway for a seven-year stint as a research scientist for the Norwegian Polar Institute. Derocher served as the chair for the International Union for Conservation of Nature's Polar Bear Specialist Group from 2005 to 2009 and is still a member. This group provides information on polar bear research and management to decision makers in government. Derocher currently works as a professor of biological sciences at the University of Alberta.

In 2004, Derocher co-authored a paper on the effects of global warming on polar bear populations. In the paper, Derocher and his colleagues argued that warmer Arctic temperatures are melting the sea ice polar bears rely on as their primary habitat. The paper was a major influence that led the U.S. government to list the polar bear as a threatened species in 2008.

Staying Warm

Many animals in tundra ecosystems have thick fur coats, extra layers of fat, or feathers to keep them warm. In this activity, you can see how having these extra layers help tundra animals stay warm.

Materials

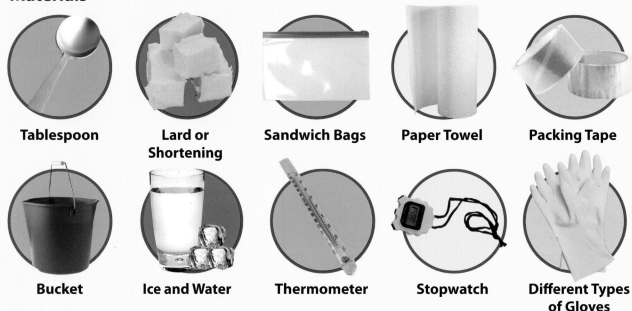

Tablespoon	Lard or Shortening	Sandwich Bags	Paper Towel	Packing Tape

Bucket	Ice and Water	Thermometer	Stopwatch	Different Types of Gloves

1. Scoop a large amount of lard or shortening into a sandwich bag.

2. Turn another sandwich bag inside out. Place this bag inside the bag of lard or shortening. Line up the top of both bags.

3. Using paper towel, wipe the tops of both bags clean. Then, tape the tops closed, leaving a small opening for your hand.

4. Fill the bucket with water. Use the thermometer to measure the temperature of the water. Add ice until the temperature is between 48° and 64°F (9° and 18°C).

5. Place your bare hand in the ice water. Use the stopwatch to time how long you can keep your hand in the water.

6. Next, repeat the experiment wearing different gloves. For each glove, time how long you can keep your hand in the water.

7. Finally, put your hand inside the bag of lard or shortening. How long can you keep your hand in the water? Which covering kept your hand warmest?

Create a Food Web

U se this book, and research on the Internet, to create a food web of tundra ecosystem plants and animals. Start by finding at least three organisms of each type—producers, primary consumers, secondary consumers, and tertiary consumers. Then, begin linking these organisms together into food chains. Draw the arrows of each food chain in a different color. Use a **red** pen or crayon for one food chain and **green** and **blue** for the others. You should find that many of these food chains connect, creating a food web. Add the rest of the arrows to complete the food web using a pencil or **black** pen.

Once your food web is complete, use it to answer the following questions.

1 How would removing one organism from your food web affect the other organisms in the web?

2 What would happen to the rest of the food web if the producers were taken away?

3 How would decomposers fit into the food web?

Sample Food Web

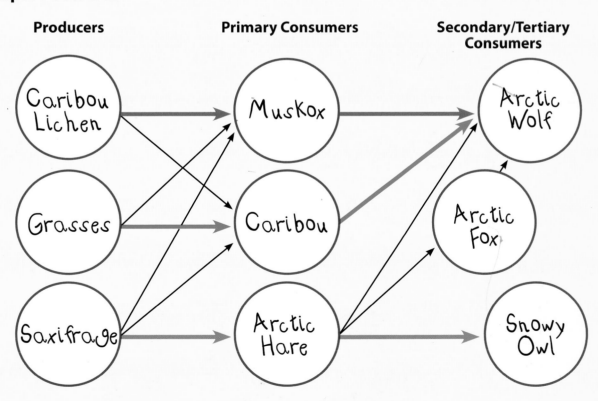

Producers	Primary Consumers	Secondary/Tertiary Consumers
Caribou Lichen	Muskox	Arctic Wolf
Grasses	Caribou	Arctic Fox
Saxifrage	Arctic Hare	Snowy Owl

1. What is an ecosystem?

2. Are there tundra regions on all of Earth's continents?

3. How much of Earth's land area is covered by tundra?

4. What is a glacier?

5. What are pingos? How do they form?

6. What are weather balloons used for in the tundra?

7. What is lichen?

8. How do people in the tundra use Arctic cotton?

9. What tundra animal is the largest carnivore that lives on land?

10. What are the three biggest threats to animals that live in tundra ecosystems?

Answers

1. A region within Earth's biosphere where plants and animals form a community

2. No. Arctic Tundra is found in Europe, Asia, North America, and Antarctica. However, alpine tundra can be found on high mountain peaks on all continents except Australia.

3. About 20 percent

4. A slow-moving mass of snow and ice

5. Pingos are mound-shaped structures. They form when layers of plants freeze and build up on top of each other.

6. Weather balloons measure gas levels in the atmosphere.

7. An organism made up of fungi and algae

8. To line their boots, gloves, and other clothing

9. The polar bear

10. Hunting, pollution, and global warming

Glossary

algae: organisms that can make their own food, similar to plants

altitudes: the height of something in relation to sea level or ground level

anthropology: the study of humans and their customs

Arctic Circle: the area around the northernmost part of the globe

axis: an imaginary line around which an object rotates

biome: a large area where certain kinds of plants and animals can be found; can include more than one ecosystem

bogs: spongy, damp land

ecosystems: communities of living things sharing an environment

endangered: in danger of becoming extinct

fungi: organisms that get their food from decomposing plants or animals

global warming: the increase in the average temperature in recent years

greenhouse gases: atmospheric gases that can reflect heat back to Earth

hemisphere: one of two halves of Earth

hibernate: to spend winter resting or sleeping to save energy

migrate: to move from one place to another; especially at regular times of year, according to the seasons

nutrients: substances that feed plants or animals

organic: materials that come from living things

organisms: living things

paleontology: the study of fossils

photosynthesis: the process in which a green plant uses sunlight to change water and carbon dioxide into food for itself

pollen: a yellow powder made by flowers

regurgitated: to spit up

species: a group of similar plants and animals that can mate together

Index

Log on to www.av2books.com

AV² by Weigl brings you media enhanced books that support active learning. Go to www.av2books.com, and enter the special code found on page 2 of this book. You will gain access to enriched and enhanced content that supplements and complements this book. Content includes video, audio, weblinks, quizzes, a slide show, and activities.

Audio
Listen to sections of the book read aloud.

Video
Watch informative video clips.

Embedded Weblinks
Gain additional information for research.

Try This!
Complete activities and hands-on experiments.

WHAT'S ONLINE?

Try This!	Embedded Weblinks	Video	EXTRA FEATURES
Complete an activity to test your knowledge of the levels of organization in a tundra ecosystem.	Find out more information on tundra ecosystems.	Watch a video about tundra ecosystems.	**Audio** Listen to sections of the book read aloud.
Complete an activity to test your knowledge of energy pyramids.	Learn more about the animals that live in tundra ecosystems.	Watch a video about animals that live in tundra ecosystems.	**Key Words** Study vocabulary, and complete a matching word activity.
Create a timeline of important events in tundra ecosystems.	Find out more about the plants that grow in tundra ecosystems.		**Slide Show** View images and captions, and prepare a presentation.
Write a biography about a scientist.	Read about current research in tundra ecosystems.		**Quizzes** Test your knowledge.
	Learn more about threats facing tundra ecosystems.		

AV² was built to bridge the gap between print and digital. We encourage you to tell us what you like and what you want to see in the future.

Sign up to be an AV² Ambassador at www.av2books.com/ambassador.